Kwanzaa

Why We Celebrate It the Way We Do

by Martin Hintz and Kate Hintz

CAPSTONE PRESS
MANKATO

C A P S T O N E   P R E S S

818 North Willow Street • Mankato, MN 56001

Library of Congress Cataloging-in-Publication Data
Hintz, Martin.
   Kwanzaa : why we celebrate it the way we do / by Martin and Kate Hintz.
   p. cm. -- (Celebrate series)
   Includes bibliographical references and index.
   Summary: Discusses the origins and symbols of Kwanzaa, the holiday that focuses on African American history, culture, and experiences, and offers suggestions for ways to celebrate this holiday.
   ISBN 1-56065-329-9
1. Kwanzaa--Juvenile literature. 2. Afro-Americans--Social life and customs--Juvenile literature. 3. United States--Social life and customs--Juvenile literature. [1. Kwanzaa. 2. Afro-Americans--Social life and customs.] I. Hintz, Kate. II. Title. III. Series.
GT4403.H55   1996
394.2'61--dc20   95-45616
                                                         CIP
                                                         AC

Photo credits
International Stock Photography/Dusty Willison, 4, 37; James Davis, 18
Archive Photos, 7, 38
Silver Image, 8, 21
Patented Photos, 12, 16, 26, 29, 34
FPG International/Tom Wilson, 15
Bill Eilers, 22, 24, 35
Peter Ford, 30, 32, 42
The Children's Museum, 40

Table of Contents

Words in **boldface** type in the text are defined
in the Glossary in the back of this book.

Chapter 1

A Different Kind of Holiday

A special holiday called Kwanzaa celebrates the African culture. Blacks all over the world take part in this holiday.

Kwanzaa is not religious. It does not celebrate an event. It celebrates a whole race of people.

In some ways, Kwanzaa is like other holidays. People celebrating Kwanzaa give gifts like at Christmas. They make vows like at New Year's. They have a feast with harvested food like at Thanksgiving. Candles are used as symbols like at Hanukkah. A flag is important like at the Fourth of July.

Kwanzaa is all about taking pride in African heritage.

What Is Kwanzaa?

Kwanzaa is held for seven days, from December 26 to January 1. The days of Kwanzaa are observed at home by families.

Seven is an important number in Kwanzaa. There are seven days of celebrating. There are seven symbols on the table. There are seven principles to think about and live by. The word Kwanzaa has seven letters.

Families pass on family traditions and treasures during Kwanzaa. Everyone thinks of where they come from and how they want to live.

A Special Flag

In the early 1900s, Marcus Garvey made a flag. Garvey was an African-American leader. He called his flag the **bendera ya taifa**. The bendera had three stripes. A black stripe was for the color of his people. A red stripe was for their struggle. A green stripe meant the future.

The flag's connection to the African homeland gave blacks a sense of identity. They were proud to fly the bendera. Having roots was important to them. Pride in the African **heritage** was growing.

Marcus Garvey was an African-American leader. He created the bendera, a flag that gave blacks a sense of identity.

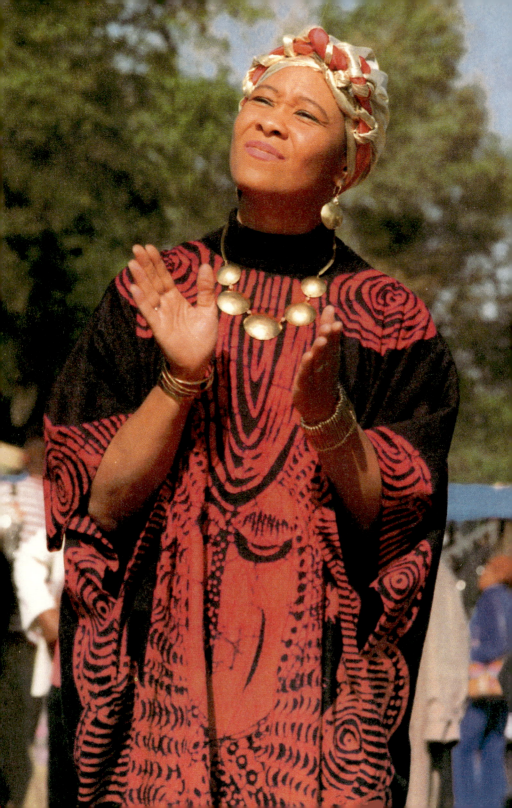

Chapter 2
Starting Kwanzaa

Africa has always been a center of
education and culture. In ancient times, Egypt,
Ghana, and Mali were great kingdoms.

Important kings and queens, warriors, poets,
astronomers, and builders of cities lived in
these kingdoms. People used art, dance, and
music to express themselves. Caravans loaded
with riches traveled across the deserts and
grasslands.

People from every part of Africa made
wonderful contributions to the arts and

**Celebrating an African holiday helps African Americans
remember their culture. This woman is wearing African
kente cloth.**

sciences. Their traditions were kept alive by storytellers.

When Africans were brought to North America as slaves, many of these traditions were set aside. Africans could not express themselves freely.

Renewal of Cultural Ways

Dr. Maulana Karenga saw that African Americans needed to renew their cultural ways. He wanted African Americans to be proud.

Karenga was an African-American activist. An activist is a person who writes and speaks about what he or she believes. Karenga wrote articles about black culture. He spoke everywhere he could. He gave speeches at universities. He attended business meetings. He spoke to politicians.

In 1966, Karenga suggested that African Americans have a holiday of their own. It would not be political or religious like many holidays. This holiday was to be a cultural celebration. Celebrating an African holiday would help African Americans remember their culture.

Karenga called the holiday Kwanzaa. It is a word from the East African language of Swahili. It means "first" or "first fruits of the harvest."

Joining People Together

Karenga wanted Kwanzaa to link African Americans with all African people. He wanted African Americans to feel close to their black brothers and sisters all over the world. The holiday would remind black people everywhere of their ongoing fight for dignity, justice, and peace.

Family gatherings and ceremonies in honor of the harvest are still important in Africa. They are also major parts of Kwanzaa. In some ways, Kwanzaa is like a harvest festival.

Kwanzaa does not replace Christmas or New Year's celebrations. Many African-American families enjoy traditions from several cultures. Some children put red, black, and green African decorations on their Christmas trees.

Chapter 3
Kwanzaa Symbols

S ymbols are an important part of the Kwanzaa holiday. A symbol is something that stands for another thing. At Kwanzaa, symbols are used to focus attention on the holiday's meaning. There are seven symbols of Kwanzaa.

Mkeka and Kinara

The **mkeka** (em-kay-kah) is a place mat. It can be made from straw, cloth, or paper. It is

There are seven symbols of Kwanzaa that focus on the holiday's meaning.

black, red, and green, the same colors as the bendera. The mkeka stands for tradition and for the past. The other symbols rest on the mkeka, just like everything rests on the traditions of the past.

The **kinara** (kee-nah-rah) is a candleholder with places for seven candles. It stands for the African people who are the ancestors of African Americans.

Mishumaa Saba

The seven candles are called **mishumaa saba** (mee-shu-mah sah-bah). They stand for the seven principles of Kwanzaa.

The middle candle is black. Three candles are green. They are placed on the right side of the holder. Three candles are red. They are placed on the left side.

The black candle is the first to be lighted. On the second day, the red candle next to the black will be lighted. On the third day, the green candle next to the black is lighted. On each new day of Kwanzaa, an additional candle

A candle is lighted on each of the seven days of Kwanzaa.

is lighted. Switching from red to green is
important. It reminds people that struggle
comes first, then come rewards.

The kuumba principle encourages people to use their talents alone or in a group.

Kikombe Cha Umoja and Mazao

Kikombe cha umoja (kee-kom-bay cha oo-moh-jah) is a cup from which everyone in the family drinks. It is the unity cup. It stands for staying together.

16

Mazao are placed on the mkeka. Mazao are the fruits and vegetables of the harvest. They represent the hard work and cooperation of the year. When the mazao are put on the table, they honor people and their work.

Muhindi and Zawadi

An ear of corn is set out for each child in the family. The corn is called **muhindi** (moo-hin-dee). This symbol is used even if a family has no children. Then it symbolizes the children who will be born. It also symbolizes all the African children in the world.

Zawadi (zah-wah-dee) are wrapped gifts for children. Parents like to give gifts that tell about their African heritage. Sometimes the gifts are handmade. Sometimes they are inexpensive gifts like books, tapes of African music, or subscriptions to African-American magazines. The gifts are given to the children as a reward for keeping promises they made during the year.

17

Chapter 4
Principles of Kwanzaa

The seven principles of Kwanzaa are called the **nguzo saba** (en-goo-zoh sah-bah). A principle is a rule or an important truth. People try to live up to each principle.

Each day of Kwanzaa is dedicated to one of the seven principles. At the beginning of the day, one person greets the others by saying, "Habari gani?" This means, "what is the news?" The answer is the principle celebrated that day.

Umoja

The first principle is **umoja** (oo-moh-jah). It means unity. People should work hard to keep

Family is an important part of Kwanzaa.

their family and community together. An example of umoja is not fighting with your brother or sister. Arguing keeps people apart. Umoja is about staying together.

Kujichagulia

The second principle is **kujichagulia** (koo-gee-cha-goo-lee-yah). It means self-determination. You can decide who you are and who you want to be. No one else decides for you.

People use this day of Kwanzaa to learn traditions that help define who they are. They learn ways to identify with their culture. People may learn special ways to braid hair, or they may study African-American heroes.

Ujima

The third principle is **ujima** (oo-gee-mah). This means collective work and responsibility. Everyone should work together to make a stronger community. People should share their problems with other people. They should let others share problems with them. People should solve problems together.

One principle of Kwanzaa says you define who you are.

There are many things you can do to help others. You can help an elderly neighbor in the garden. You could start a food collection at school. You can give the food to a shelter for the homeless.

Ujima is also working together as a family. This third day of Kwanzaa is the perfect time to do a family project. Families could paint a room or clean out the garage. They could build something, like a chair or bookcase for their house. The important thing is being together as a family while doing a job that helps everyone.

Ujamaa

The fourth principle is **ujamaa** (oo-jah-mah). It means cooperative economics. African Americans should set up their own businesses and **patronize** other African-American stores. Buying from each other is a good way to make a community strong.

Derrick Martin, a University of Minnesota student, started his own T-shirt company. He designs and sells the *Love Sees No Color* T-shirts.

Some families honor ujamaa by paying for their children to go to college. After college, the children can come back to their neighborhood and contribute to their community.

Cooperative economics also means saving as a family. Families save their money to buy a gift the whole family can share. The gift can be something that is needed or something for fun.

Nia

The fifth principle is **nia** (nee-yah). It means purpose in life. On this day, people think about their actions and the consequences of their actions. Everything that they do should be done for a reason.

Everyone should have a purpose or goal for his or her life. People use this day of Kwanzaa to dream about what they want to accomplish. This is a good time to study important African-American leaders. People who did great things can inspire others to do a great thing, too.

Some goals might be small. A goal might be to keep promises or to do one nice thing every day.

Kuumba

The sixth principle is **kuumba** (koo-oom-bah). It means creativity.

This principle encourages people to use all of their talents. They should do the best they can while studying or working at a job.

Thinking of better ways to do things is also kuumba. People can use their ideas to create stories, new dances, or colorful clothes that show their heritage.

Imani

The seventh principle is **imani** (ee-mah-nee). Imani means faith. People can have faith in themselves, in their parents, in their teachers, and in their race. Imani means that African Americans are important and valuable. The other six principles of Kwanzaa are empty without faith.

Kwanzaa is a good time to study African-American leaders, such as Jesse Jackson.

Chapter 5
Celebrating Karamu

On December 31, families celebrating Kwanzaa have a huge dinner. This is called **karamu** (kah-rah-moo). Karamu means feast. Family and friends greet each other by saying, "Kwanzaa yenu iwe na heri." This means "May your Kwanzaa be happy."

Weeks are spent planning and preparing for karamu. Working together to prepare for karamu is an important part of the celebration.

During karamu, the Kwanzaa feast, people get together and talk about the importance of Kwanzaa.

Karamu can be held in a house, a community center, or anywhere there is room for many people. Decorations are mostly red, green, and black. Families invite others who may not have relatives nearby to join them. They make these guests feel welcome. They are part of the African-American community.

Food, Family, and Fun

Almost everyone brings food to karamu. But it is all right if someone cannot bring anything. The dinner is for sharing.

Somebody might bring jolof rice. This dish is from West Africa. It is made with chicken, peppers, and tomatoes. Another person might bring pork roast adobo. This is a spicy dish from the Caribbean. Another visitor might bring black-eyed pea salad. It might be a family recipe handed down from a great-grandma.

The guests lay their gifts of food on the mkeka. Everyone helps themselves to a plate.

All the chairs, sofas, benches, and stools are filled. Some people sit on pillows on the floor. No one minds being crowded. Having fun with friends and relatives is part of Kwanzaa. It shows community spirit.

After eating, dishes are washed and put away. Everyone gathers around in a group. They sing songs. They read poems. Sometimes they dance.

After the feast, people gather to tell stories, read poems, sing songs, and dance.

When everyone goes home, they are tired. But they are ready to face the new year.

Celebrate All Year Long

Kwanzaa does not have to be celebrated just once a year. Some families display a Kwanzaa

To make a Kwanzaa altar, families place the Kwanzaa symbols together on a table.

altar all year long. It reminds them to live by the seven principles.

To make a Kwanzaa altar, families place the Kwanzaa symbols on a table in a corner of the living room. A poster describing the seven principles is hung on a wall nearby. The family then works hard every day to keep these ideas and values alive. If the children keep their promises, they will receive zawadi presents at the next Kwanzaa.

Chapter 6

Activities for Kwanzaa

Y ou want Kwanzaa to be better and better every year. Getting ready takes time. There are many things you can do to plan and prepare.

Tell Your Friends

Your friends might want to learn about Kwanzaa. You can explain what the holiday means. Do not be nervous. Start by saying, "Hujambo." This means "good morning" or "hello."

Tell your friends about Kwanzaa and what it means. You can help them plan their own Kwanzaa celebration.

You can organize a school assembly. The best time is just before Kwanzaa begins. This helps people remember to celebrate Kwanzaa. Play some African music. Show some African crafts.

Help others plan their own ceremony. Remember kujichagulia, the self-determination principle. Speak for yourself. Tell your friends why Kwanzaa is important to blacks.

The official Kwanzaa holiday is held from December 26 to January 1, but some people celebrate it all year long.

Law professor Anita Hill displays the imani principle by having faith in herself.

Plan School Activities

Ask your social studies teacher if you can bring a mkeka, kikombe, muhindi, and kinara to school. Explain the meaning of the mat, cup, corn, and candleholder. Light the candles while telling everyone about the importance of the seven principles. Be ready to answer questions.

A display of Kwanzaa symbols can be set up in the school library or in a display case in the hall. Ask local travel agents for colorful posters of Africa. They may be able to lend or give them to you.

Is there someone in your area who has been to Africa? Do you know someone in business who has an office in an African country? Are there African students at a nearby college or university? Invite them to your school.

These people can tell you and your friends what living in Africa is like. They may have suggestions on how to celebrate African holidays. Invite them to your Kwanzaa. You might write to someone they know in Africa.

Read Books

Your teacher or librarian might be able to suggest books to read. The stories can be about Kwanzaa. Or they can be about the African-American experience. Or they can be about Africa.

Learn as much as you can about African culture. This will help you appreciate Kwanzaa even more. Then tell your family what you learned. They will be excited to hear it.

Be Creative

Help decorate your house or your classroom for Kwanzaa. Use plenty of green, red, and black. Make something yourself. Anything that

Africa has always been a center of education and culture.

shows your heritage can be a decoration for the holiday.

Make some jewelry out of shells or beads. Create an African mask. Try to find some **kente** cloth. Kente is made in West Africa. Women make dresses and decorations with it.

Write a story or a poem about Kwanzaa or your family. It can be about anything at all. All of these things show kuumba, the creativity principle.

Trace Your Heritage

How far back can your trace your family? Searching for your roots is called **genealogy.** Trace your own heritage. Ask your family members if they remember their grandparents and great-grandparents.

Make a **family tree**. Everyone's name is a branch. Be sure you list your own name. Save the chart and add to it as you get more

Alex Haley wrote the book, *Roots*, that tells the history of an African-American family.

information. When you grow up and have children, this family tree can be a zawadi gift.

Make a Mkeka

One way to be creative is to make your own mkeka, the Kwanzaa place mat. You will need

The symbols of Kwanzaa include the Kwanzaa mat, the unity cup, and fruits and vegetables.

scissors, glue, and large sheets of red, green, and black construction paper.

Cut one piece of paper into one-inch (2.5 centimeter) strips. Do not cut all the way to the end. Leave one inch (2.5 centimeters) along one of the long sides of the paper. The strips will hold together, and the paper will look like a grass skirt.

Cut the other two pieces of paper into one-inch (2.5 centimeter) strips the long way. This time, cut all the way through.

Take one of these long strips and begin to weave it through your grass skirt. Go over the first strip. Go under the second strip. Weave the strip back and forth until you get to the end.

Now weave a second strip. Use a different color. This time start by going under the first strip and over the second strip.

Keep weaving until you run out of room. Then glue the ends together so they will not slip out. You have made your own mkeka.

Glossary

bendera ya taifa—African-American flag
family tree—chart listing relatives
genealogy—tracing ancestors
heritage—things handed down from ancestors
imani—faith
karamu—feast
kente—brightly colored African cloth
kikombe cha umoja—ceremonial cup
kinara—candleholder
Kwanzaa—Swahili word for first or first fruits
kujichagulia—self-determination
kuumba—creativity
mazao—fruits and vegetables of the harvest

Be creative. You can follow the principle of kuumba and make your own Kwanzaa crafts.

mishumaa saba—the seven candles of Kwanzaa

mkeka—place mat

muhindi—ear of corn

nguzo saba—the seven principles of Kwanzaa

nia—purpose in life

patronize—visit or use a business

symbol—something that stands for another thing

ujamaa—using money for the good of the community

ujima—collective work and responsibility

umoja—unity

zawadi—Kwanzaa gifts

To Learn More

Chocolate, Deborah M. Newton. *Kwanzaa.* Chicago: Children's Press, 1990.

Copage, Eric V. *Kwanzaa: An African-American Celebration of Culture and Cooking.* New York: William Morrow, 1991.

McClester, Cedric. *Kwanzaa: Everything You Always Wanted to Know But Didn't Know Where to Ask.* New York: Gumbs & Thomas, 1994.

Pinkney, Andrea Davis. *Seven Candles for Kwanzaa.* New York: Dial Books, 1993.

Porter, A.P. *Kwanzaa.* Minneapolis: Carolrhoda Books, 1991.

Useful Addresses

Armistad Research Center
Tulane University
6823 St. Charles Avenue
New Orleans, LA 70118

America's Black Holocaust Museum
2233 North Fourth Street
Milwaukee, WI 53212

Congress of Racial Equality
1457 Flatbush Avenue
Brooklyn, NY 11210

**National Association for the Advancement of
  Colored People**
4805 Mount Hope Drive
Baltimore, MD 21215

Wisconsin Black Historical Society
2620 West Center Street
Milwaukee, WI 53206

You can read about the black experience in *Harambee* and *Skipping Stones* magazines.

Index